TREAT

TREAT

50 RECIPES FOR
NO-BAKE MARSHMALLOW TREATS

STEPHANIE BANYAS

CLARKSON POTTER/PUBLISHERS

NEW YORK

Copyright © 2015 by
Clarkson Potter/Publishers
Photographs copyright © 2015 by
Davide Luciano

Published in the United States by
Clarkson Potter/Publishers, an imprint
of the Crown Publishing Group, a
division of Penguin Random House LLC,
New York. www.clarksonpotter.com

CLARKSON POTTER is a trademark
and POTTER with colophon is a
registered trademark of Penguin
Random House LLC.

Library of Congress Cataloging-in-
Publication Data
Banyas, Stephanie.
Treat / Stephanie Banyas, Clarkson
Potter.—First edition. Includes index.
1. Candy 2. Chocolate candy. I. Title.
TX791.B28 2015
641.85'3—dc23   2015001621

ISBN 978-0-8041-8685-8
eBook ISBN 978-0-8041-8686-5

Printed in China

Cover design by Yeon Kim
Cover photograph by Brian Kennedy

10 9 8 7 6 5 4 3 2 1

First Edition

ACKNOWLEDGMENTS

MY PARENTS, Rose and George Banyas, for their love and support. I am so lucky to have you.

RICA ALLANNIC, for opening new doors for me.

ASHLEY PHILLIPS, for taking a chance on me and being a great and patient editor!

Last but not least, **BOBBY FLAY**—without you, none of this would be possible.

CONTENTS

INTRODUCTION

Hooray for treats! A childhood favorite for most Americans, these crunchy, gooey sweets never go out of style—they're served frequently at children's birthday parties and even weddings. The original recipe for the marshmallow crisp rice cereal treat was created back in 1928 by a team of home economics teachers who developed a simple no-bake cookie. They dubbed the confection "Krispies Marshmallow Squares," and the treats became an instant classic.

Popular among adults and kids alike, these delicious sweets are perfect for bringing to parties and school functions, and they make a quick snack or dessert. Plus, it's easy to prepare a gluten-free version: Just check the label of the cereal before you buy it. It's hard to believe these treats are more popular today than when they were introduced almost 90 years ago—and that you can find them in almost 100 varieties. The sky's the limit for flavor combinations and mix-ins, so let your imagination run wild. The recipes in this book were inspired by all sorts of favorite desserts, from candy bars and cookies to ice cream flavors and confections. The recipes are designed for you to play with, so try adding different ingredients, and check out the sidebar, opposite, for some fun ideas. And if you're feeling extra gourmet, you can make your own marshmallows. There are recipes for ten flavors of homemade marshmallows that taste scrumptious and will add an extra special touch to your finished product.

Cute, fun, and oh-so-easy to make, treats are a perfect go-to sweet—and sure to be a hit with any crowd.

TREAT TIPS

Rice cereal treat recipes are easy to prepare but can be extremely messy while doing so. Here are a few suggestions for making the best treats possible.

THE CEREAL

Although they originated as treats made with Rice Krispies, you can use any puffed rice cereal in these recipes. If you want to be more adventurous, try other types of cereal—Froot Loops, Count Chocula, Cap'n Crunch, Cheerios; the different textures and flavors will make for some delicious alternatives.

THE PAN

Use a nonstick baking dish that you have liberally buttered or coated with nonstick spray. If you don't have a nonstick pan, line your baking dish with parchment paper and lightly coat it with nonstick cooking spray. One benefit of using parchment paper is that you can lift the treats out of the tray easily when it's time to cut them.

THE POT

A large nonstick stockpot (6 or 8 quarts) works best for melting the butter and marshmallows. A nonstick surface is essential, as a pan with melted, dried marshmallow in it is next to impossible to get clean. For extra protection, I lightly coat the pot with nonstick spray. The marshmallow mixture comes out easily, and cleanup is a breeze.

MIXING IT UP

The original treats recipe is a blank canvas for flavors. Almost anything works, so have fun mixing and matching. Here are a few suggestions for yummy things to toss in.

1 Flavored marshmallows can add great color and flavor. Recipes for making your own start on page 13, or buy them at the grocery store or online.

2 Pure extracts, such as vanilla or almond, can enhance flavor considerably.

3 Dried cranberries, raisins, coconut, chocolate chips, chopped candy bars, crushed cookies, or chopped nuts are delicious additions.

4 Melt a little peanut butter or other nut butter along with the marshmallows.

5 Mix in caramel or chocolate toppings, or drizzle some on top.

6 Stir finely grated citrus zest into the melted marshmallow mixture to add a punch of natural flavor.

THE MARSHMALLOW MIXTURE

Working with melted marshmallow can be a sticky mess. Use a rubber spatula, coated with nonstick cooking spray, to scrape the mixture into the prepared dish. To press the mixture into the dish, either push on it with your hands and a piece of wax paper or press down with a heavily greased spatula. Always let the mixture cool for at least 15 minutes before cutting, so the treats firm up and become less messy. Use a sharp knife or pizza cutter to slice into squares.

STORING TREATS

My versions of these treats contain more butter and marshmallow than the original recipe. This means the treats are creamier than usual, and they will keep longer. If you are able to refrain from eating a whole pan of treats in one day, here are few simple guidelines that will ensure your treats will taste just as delicious as when you first prepare them.

1 Start with fresh ingredients. Check the expiration date on your cereal, butter, marshmallows, and any additional items.

2 Store cooled treats in an airtight container at room temperature for up to two days. Choose a container large enough to store all of your treats but small enough to leave very little excess room. The more open space left in the container, the more the treats are exposed to air, which will dry out and harden your goodies.

3 Put a sheet of parchment or wax paper on the bottom of the container, and place a piece in between each layer of treats to prevent them from sticking together.

HOW TO MELT CHOCOLATE

Melting chocolate seems easy, but how you go about it will affect your end result. Here are three methods for melting chocolate effectively.

For each method, start by breaking or cutting the chocolate into small (½-inch) pieces for even melting. Make sure your work surface, pans, and tools are absolutely dry, as added moisture may cause the chocolate to thicken. Melt it slowly. Chocolate burns easily, so be careful not to apply too much heat.

Double Boiler Method: Put the chocolate in the top pan of a double boiler set over hot, but not boiling, water. You can also use a tempered-glass or metal mixing bowl on top of a saucepan half full of water. Melt the chocolate, stirring occasionally, until smooth.

Stovetop Method: You can use this method if you are adding chocolate to a batter. Do not use for dipping or molding. Put the chocolate in a saucepan set over very low heat. Heat the chocolate, stirring constantly, until small lumps remain. Remove the pan from the heat and stir until smooth.

Microwave Method: Put the chocolate in a microwave-safe container and heat it in a microwave oven at medium power (50 percent) for 1 to 1½ minutes. Stir. If the chocolate has not melted, heat it for 1 to 1½ more minutes, stirring every 30 seconds to avoid scorching, until small lumps remain. Remove the bowl from the microwave and stir until smooth.

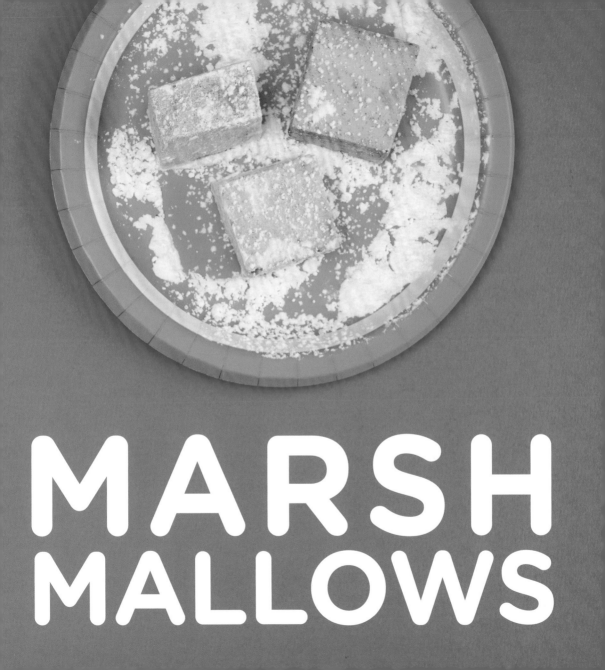

MARSH
MALLOWS

VANILLA
MARSHMALLOWS

Marshmallows found on grocery store shelves are pretty good; gourmet brands (found in specialty stores, bakeries, and online) are really good. But homemade marshmallows made in your very own kitchen are amazing. They have a super light texture and seem to just melt in your mouth. It takes a bit of time and practice to get a feel for making marshmallows, but the results are so worth it. Watching sugar and gelatin turn into fluffy, white, pillow-like confections in minutes still amazes me. • **MAKES 30 MARSHMALLOWS (22 OUNCES)**

Nonstick cooking spray

3 (¼-ounce) packages unflavored gelatin

1 cup cold water

1½ cups granulated sugar

1 cup light corn syrup

¼ teaspoon kosher salt

1 tablespoon pure vanilla extract or
1 teaspoon pure vanilla extract and
1 vanilla bean, seeds scraped

1¼ cups confectioners' sugar, for dusting

1 Line a 9 x 13-inch baking dish with foil. Coat the foil lightly with nonstick cooking spray.

2 In the bowl of an electric mixer fitted with the whisk attachment, combine the gelatin and ½ cup cold water. Let stand while you make the sugar syrup.

3 In a heavy small saucepan set over medium heat, combine the granulated sugar, corn syrup, salt, and ½ cup water. Cook, stirring and brushing down the sides of the pan with a wet pastry brush, until the sugar dissolves, about 2 minutes. Increase the heat to high and cook without stirring until the syrup reaches 240°F on a candy thermometer, about 8 minutes. Remove the pan from the heat.

RECIPE CONTINUES

4 With the mixer on low speed, slowly pour the sugar syrup into the dissolved gelatin (avoid pouring syrup onto the whisk, as it may splash). Gradually increase mixer speed to high and beat until the mixture is very thick and stiff, about 15 minutes. Add the vanilla and beat well, about 30 seconds.

5 Scrape the marshmallow mixture into the prepared dish. Smooth the top with a wet spatula or your fingers, and dust with confectioners' sugar. Let stand uncovered at room temperature until firm and slightly dried out, at least 8 hours and up to 24 hours.

6 Dust a cutting board with confectioners' sugar. Turn out the marshmallow onto the board. Dust the marshmallow with confectioners' sugar. Coat a large sharp knife with nonstick cooking spray and cut the marshmallows into 1½-inch squares. The marshmallows can be stored in an airtight container for up to two weeks.

VARIATIONS

Orange-Scented: Decrease the vanilla extract to 1 teaspoon and add the finely grated zest of 1 large orange with the vanilla.

Lime-Scented: Decrease the vanilla extract to 1 teaspoon and add the finely grated zest of 2 limes with the vanilla.

Gingerbread-Scented: Substitute ¼ cup molasses for ¼ cup of the corn syrup, and add ¼ teaspoon ground cinnamon, ¼ teaspoon ground ginger, ⅛ teaspoon ground cloves, and ⅛ teaspoon ground nutmeg.

STRAWBERRY
MARSHMALLOWS

Adding strawberry puree to the basic vanilla marshmallow recipe makes pink-hued sweets that taste like a creamy milkshake full of berry flavor. Substitute your favorite berry or fruit flavor puree to make a colorful variety! • **MAKES 30 MARSHMALLOWS (22 OUNCES)**

Nonstick cooking spray

½ cup strawberry puree

½ cup plus 2 tablespoons cold water

½ teaspoon red gel food coloring

3 (¼-ounce) packets unflavored gelatin

2 cups granulated sugar

⅔ cup light corn syrup

⅛ teaspoon fine sea salt

2 tablespoons pure vanilla extract

¾ cup confectioners' sugar

¼ cup cornstarch

1 Line a 9 x 13-inch baking dish with foil. Coat the foil with nonstick cooking spray.

2 In the bowl of an electric mixer fitted with the whisk attachment, combine the strawberry puree, 2 tablespoons of the cold water, and the red food coloring. Sprinkle the gelatin over the liquid. Let stand until the gelatin softens, at least 10 minutes.

3 In a heavy medium saucepan set over medium-low heat, combine the granulated sugar, corn syrup, salt, and remaining ½ cup cold water. Cook, stirring and brushing down the sides of the pan with a wet pastry brush, until the sugar dissolves, 2 minutes. Increase the heat to high and bring the syrup to a boil. Cook, without

RECIPE CONTINUES

stirring, until the syrup reaches 240°F on a candy thermometer, about 8 minutes. Remove the pan from the heat.

4 With the mixer on low speed, slowly pour the hot syrup into the gelatin mixture in a thin stream down the side of the bowl (avoid pouring syrup onto the whisk, as it may splash). Gradually increase mixer speed to high and beat until the mixture is very thick and stiff, about 10 minutes. Add the vanilla and beat well, about 30 seconds.

5 Scrape the marshmallow mixture into the prepared dish. Smooth the top with a wet spatula or your fingers. Let stand uncovered at room temperature until firm and slightly dried out, at least 8 hours and up to 24 hours.

6 Sift together the confectioners' sugar and cornstarch. Cover a work surface with wax paper, then liberally dust with the sugar mixture. Turn out the marshmallow onto the work surface and peel off the foil. Dust the marshmallow with the sugar mixture. Coat a large sharp knife with nonstick cooking spray and cut the marshmallows into 1½-inch squares. Toss each marshmallow in the remaining sugar mixture to coat. The marshmallows can be stored in an airtight container for up to two weeks.

VARIATIONS

Blueberry: Substitute blueberry puree for strawberry.

Raspberry: Substitute raspberry puree for strawberry.

Peach: Substitute peach puree for strawberry.

CHOCOLATE
MARSHMALLOWS

Chocolate marshmallows look like rich, dark velvet. Bite into one and it's almost like eating a chocolate cloud! Cocoa powder gives these marshmallows their rich chocolaty flavor.

• **MAKES 30 MARSHMALLOWS (22 OUNCES)**

Nonstick cooking spray

1⅓ cups water

⅓ cup plus ½ cup Dutch-processed cocoa powder

3 (¼-ounce) packets unflavored gelatin

2 cups granulated sugar

¾ cup light corn syrup

1 tablespoon pure vanilla extract

½ cup confectioners' sugar

2 tablespoons cornstarch

1 Line 9 x 13-inch baking dish with foil. Coat the foil liberally with nonstick cooking spray.

2 In a small saucepan set over medium heat, bring ⅓ cup water to a simmer. Add ⅓ cup of the cocoa powder and whisk until smooth.

3 Put ½ cup cold water in the bowl of a stand mixer. Sprinkle the gelatin over the water. Let stand until the gelatin softens, at least 10 minutes.

4 Add the warm cocoa mixture to the gelatin, and stir or mix on low to thoroughly combine.

5 In a heavy medium saucepan set over medium-high heat, combine the granulated sugar, corn syrup, and ½ cup water. Stir to dissolve the sugar. Cook without stirring, brushing down the sides of the pan with a wet pastry brush, until the syrup reaches 240°F on a candy thermometer, about 8 minutes. Remove the pan from the heat. While the mixture cools, briefly run the mixer on low speed once or twice until the gelatin mixture is well combined.

6 With the mixer on low speed, slowly pour the hot syrup into the gelatin mixture in a thin stream down the side of the bowl (avoid pouring syrup onto the whisk, as it may splash). Gradually increase mixer speed to high and beat until very thick and stiff, about 10 minutes. Add the vanilla and beat to blend, about 30 seconds.

7 Scrape the marshmallow mixture into the prepared dish. Smooth the top with a wet spatula or your fingers. Let stand uncovered at room temperature until firm and slightly dried out, at least 12 hours and up to 24 hours.

8 Sift together the confectioners' sugar, cornstarch, and the remaining ½ cup cocoa powder. Cover a work surface with wax paper, then dust liberally with the sugar mixture. Turn out the marshmallow onto the work surface and peel off the foil. Dust the marshmallow with the sugar mixture. Coat a large sharp knife with nonstick cooking spray, then sprinkle both sides with the sugar mixture. Cut the marshmallow into 1½-inch squares, coating the knife blade with more sugar mixture as needed. Toss the marshmallows in the remaining sugar mixture to coat. The marshmallows can be stored in an airtight container for up to two weeks.

CREAM CHEESE
MARSHMALLOWS

These marshmallows are light and fluffy and creamy and tangy, just like their namesake in block form from Philadelphia. • **MAKES 30 MARSHMALLOWS (22 OUNCES)**

½ cup **Philadelphia cream cheese, room temperature**

⅔ cup **cold water**

3 **(¼-ounce) packets unflavored gelatin**

1½ cups **granulated sugar**

1 cup **light corn syrup**

1 tablespoon **pure vanilla extract**

½ cup **confectioners' sugar**

¼ cup **cornstarch**

1 Line 9 x 13-inch baking dish with foil. Coat the foil liberally with nonstick cooking spray.

2 In an electric mixer fitted with the whisk attachment, beat the cream cheese until smooth. Add ⅓ cup of the water. Sprinkle the gelatin over the water. Let stand until the gelatin softens, at least 10 minutes.

3 In a heavy medium saucepan set over high heat, combine the granulated sugar, corn syrup, and remaining ⅓ cup water. Cook without stirring, brushing down the sides of the pan with a wet pastry brush, until it reaches 240°F on a candy thermometer, about 8 minutes. Remove the pan from the heat.

4 A few minutes before the sugar mixtures comes to temperature, beat the cream cheese and gelatin mixture until combined. With the mixer running on low speed, slowly pour the hot syrup into the gelatin mixture in a thin stream down the side of the bowl (avoid pouring syrup onto the whisk, as it may splash). Gradually increase mixer speed to high and beat until very thick and stiff, about 10 minutes. Add the vanilla and beat to blend, about 30 seconds.

5 Scrape the marshmallow mixture into the prepared dish. Smooth the top with a wet spatula or your fingers. Put the pan in the refrigerator for at least 30 minutes and up to 4 hours to set up.

6 Sift together the confectioners' sugar and cornstarch. Cover a work surface with wax paper, then dust liberally with the sugar mixture. Turn out the marshmallow onto the work surface and peel off the foil.

Coat a large sharp knife with nonstick cooking spray, then sprinkle both sides with the sugar mixture. Cut the marshmallow into 1½-inch squares, coating the knife blade with more sugar mixture as needed. Toss the marshmallows in the remaining sugar mixture to coat. The marshmallows can be stored in an airtight container for up to two weeks.

UPDATED
CLASSICS

TOASTED COCONUT
TREATS

What would happen if you combined a coconut macaroon and a treat? This recipe, that's what! If you can find coconut-flavored marshmallows at your grocery store, opt for those instead of plain marshmallows with a touch of coconut extract, which is what the recipe calls for. Drizzle with a little melted chocolate to put these over the top. • **MAKES 16 LARGE OR 24 SMALL BARS**

1 cup sweetened coconut

7 tablespoons unsalted butter

24 Vanilla Marshmallows (page 14) or 1 (16-ounce) bag store-bought marshmallows or 15 ounces marshmallow Fluff

1 teaspoon coconut extract

½ teaspoon pure vanilla extract

Pinch of sea salt

6 cups puffed rice cereal

1 Preheat the oven to 325°F.

2 Spread the coconut in an even layer on a baking sheet and toast in the oven, stirring every few minutes, until lightly golden brown, about 12 minutes. Let cool.

3 Using 1 tablespoon of the butter, grease the bottom and sides of a 9 x 13-inch glass or nonstick baking dish.

4 In a medium pan set over medium heat, melt the remaining 6 tablespoons butter. Add the marshmallows, reduce the heat to low, and cover the pan. Let stand until the marshmallows begin to soften, 2 minutes. Add the toasted coconut, coconut extract, vanilla, and salt, and stir until smooth. Fold in the cereal and stir gently.

5 Scrape the mixture into the prepared dish and spread evenly with a piece of wax paper. Let stand for 15 minutes before cutting and serving.

PEANUT BUTTER-HONEY
TREATS

Peanut butter–flavored rice cereal bars are probably second in popularity to the original recipe. To enhance the flavor, I added honey, and then put some honey-roasted nuts on top for more crunch. If you prefer a simpler treat, just omit the honey and chopped nuts.

• MAKES 16 LARGE OR 24 SMALL BARS

7 tablespoons unsalted butter

2 tablespoons clover honey

Pinch of sea salt

24 Vanilla Marshmallows (page 14) or 1 (16-ounce) bag store-bought marshmallows or 15 ounces marshmallow Fluff

½ cup creamy peanut butter, such as JIF (do not use natural peanut butter)

1 teaspoon pure vanilla extract

6 cups puffed rice cereal

½ cup honey roasted peanuts, chopped

1 Using 1 tablespoon of the butter, grease the bottom and sides of a 9 x 13-inch glass or nonstick baking dish.

2 In a medium pan set over medium heat, melt the remaining 6 tablespoons butter. Add the honey and salt and cook, stirring, for 30 seconds. Add the marshmallows, reduce the heat to low, and cover the pan. Let stand until the marshmallows begin to soften, 2 minutes. Add the peanut butter and vanilla, and stir until smooth. Fold in the cereal and stir gently.

3 Scrape the mixture into the prepared dish and spread evenly with a piece of wax paper. Sprinkle the chopped peanuts evenly over the top, lightly pressing them so that they stick. Let stand for 15 minutes before cutting and serving.

TWENTY-FIRST CENTURY
TREATS

Sometimes you can improve on an original. Here, with a bit more butter and marshmallow, we can make one amazingly creamy, dreamy treat. Welcome to the new millennium!

• MAKES 16 LARGE OR 24 SMALL BARS

7 tablespoons unsalted butter

1 vanilla bean, seeds scraped, or
   1½ teaspoons vanilla extract

Pinch of sea salt

24 Vanilla Marshmallows (page 14)
   or 1 (16-ounce) bag store-bought
   marshmallows or 15 ounces
   marshmallow Fluff

6 cups puffed rice cereal

1 Using 1 tablespoon of the butter, grease the bottom and sides of a 9 x 13-inch glass or nonstick baking dish.

2 In a medium pan set over medium heat, melt the remaining 6 tablespoons butter. Add the vanilla seeds and salt, and stir until smooth. Add the marshmallows, reduce the heat to low, and cover the pan. Let stand until the marshmallows begin to soften, 2 minutes. Fold in the cereal and stir gently.

3 Scrape the mixture into the prepared pan and spread evenly with a piece of wax paper. Let stand for 15 minutes before cutting and serving.

TWENTY-FIRST
CENTURY TREATS
(PAGE 29)

TOASTED
MARSHMALLOW TREATS

The only thing I love more than ooey gooey melted marshmallows are those that have been toasted until golden brown. Their flavor brings back memories of summer camp and time spent around a fire with friends. • MAKES 16 LARGE OR 24 SMALL BARS

24 Vanilla Marshmallows (page 14) or 1 (16-ounce) bag store-bought marshmallows
7 tablespoons unsalted butter
1 teaspoon pure vanilla extract
Pinch of sea salt
6 cups puffed rice cereal

1 Put a rack in the upper third of the oven and preheat the broiler.

2 Line a baking sheet with parchment paper. Put half the marshmallows on the baking sheet in an even layer. Broil the marshmallows until golden brown, about 40 seconds. Turn over the marshmallows and brown the other side. Remove from the oven and let cool slightly.

3 Using 1 tablespoon of the butter, grease the bottom and sides of a 9 x 13-inch glass or nonstick baking dish.

4 In a medium pan set over medium heat, melt the remaining 6 tablespoons butter. Add the remaining untoasted marshmallows, reduce the heat to low, and cover the pan. Let stand until the marshmallows begin to soften, 2 minutes. Add the vanilla and salt and stir until smooth. Add the toasted marshmallows, cover the pan, and let stand until halfway melted, 2 minutes. Fold in the cereal and stir gently.

5 Scrape the mixture into the prepared pan and spread evenly with a piece of wax paper. Let stand for 15 minutes before cutting and serving.

BISCOFF
TREATS

Nutella isn't the only European spread gaining in popularity in the United States. Biscoff spread—a peanut butter–like spread that's made of speculoos cookies (spiced butter cookies usually enjoyed around Christmas)—is rapidly gaining fans stateside. The spread is available at many grocery stores across the country, as well as online, and Trader Joe's makes a similar version called Cookie Butter. • **MAKES 16 LARGE OR 24 SMALL BARS**

7 tablespoons unsalted butter

½ cup Biscoff spread

Pinch of sea salt

24 Vanilla Marshmallows (page 14) or 1 (16-ounce) bag store-bought marshmallows or 15 ounces marshmallow Fluff

6 cups puffed rice cereal

10 speculoos cookies, crushed (optional)

1 Using 1 tablespoon of the butter, grease the bottom and sides of a 9 x 13-inch glass or nonstick baking dish.

2 In a medium pan set over medium heat, melt the remaining 6 tablespoons butter. Add the Biscoff spread and salt, and stir until smooth. Add the marshmallows, reduce the heat to low, and cover the pan. Let stand until the marshmallows begin to soften, 2 minutes. Fold in the cereal and stir gently.

3 Scrape the mixture into the prepared dish and spread evenly with a piece of wax paper. Sprinkle the crushed cookies evenly over the top, if desired. Let stand for 15 minutes before serving.

CHOCOLATE-HAZELNUT
TREATS

Enjoyed in Italy since 1940, Nutella was first imported to the United States in 1983. The popularity of Nutella has grown steadily over the years, and it is now available in grocery stores across the country. This chocolate and hazelnut spread can be found in everything from cupcakes and cookies, and is now in rice cereal treats! • **MAKES 16 LARGE OR 24 SMALL BARS**

7 tablespoons unsalted butter

24 Vanilla Marshmallows (page 14) or 1 (16-ounce) bag store-bought marshmallows or 15 ounces marshmallow Fluff

½ cup chocolate-hazelnut spread, such as Nutella

1 teaspoon pure vanilla extract

Pinch of sea salt

6 cups puffed rice cereal

TOPPING

1 cup chocolate-hazelnut spread, such as Nutella

1 tablespoon canola oil

1 cup milk chocolate chips

½ cup chopped lightly toasted hazelnuts

1 Make the treats: Using 1 tablespoon of the butter, grease the bottom and sides of a 9 x 13-inch glass or nonstick baking dish.

2 In a medium pan set over medium heat, melt the remaining 6 tablespoons butter. Add the marshmallows, reduce the heat to low, and cover the pan. Let stand until the marshmallows begin to soften, 2 minutes. Add the chocolate-hazelnut spread, vanilla, and salt, and stir until smooth. Fold in the cereal and stir gently.

3 Scrape the mixture into the prepared dish and spread evenly with a piece of wax paper. Let stand for 15 minutes.

4 Make the topping: Combine the chocolate-hazelnut spread, oil, and chocolate chips in a microwave-safe bowl and melt in the microwave or on the stovetop (see instructions on page 11). Spread the mixture evenly over the top of the treats and sprinkle with the hazelnuts. Refrigerate until topping is firm, about 1 hour, before cutting and serving.

AFTER-SCHOOL
POWER BAR TREATS

Finally, a sweet treat you can feel good about—it's packed with seeds and dried fruits. Give these to your children after school or eat them yourself after a workout. The recipe is versatile: Try swapping out any nut butter for the peanut butter, cashews and almonds for the peanuts, or dried cherries or cranberries for the raisins. • **MAKES 16 LARGE OR 24 SMALL BARS**

1 cup old-fashioned oats

3 tablespoons sesame seeds

7 tablespoons unsalted butter

**24 Vanilla Marshmallows (page 14)
or 1 (16-ounce) bag store-bought
marshmallows or 15 ounces
marshmallow Fluff**

1 teaspoon pure vanilla extract

**1 cup creamy peanut butter, such as JIF
(do not use natural peanut butter)**

4 cups puffed rice cereal

½ cup peanuts

½ cup raisins

1 In a small skillet set over low heat, combine the oats and sesame seeds and cook, stirring occasionally, until lightly toasted, about 5 minutes. Set aside.

2 Using 1 tablespoon of the butter, grease the bottom and sides of a 9 x 13-inch glass or nonstick baking dish.

3 In a medium pan set over medium heat, melt the remaining 6 tablespoons butter. Add the marshmallows, reduce the heat to low, and cover the pan. Let stand until the marshmallows soften, 2 minutes. Add the vanilla and peanut butter, and stir until smooth. Fold in the cereal, toasted oats and sesame seeds, peanuts, and raisins, and stir gently.

4 Scrape the mixture into the prepared dish and spread evenly with a piece of wax paper. Firmly press down on the mixture to make it slightly compact. Let stand for 30 minutes before cutting and serving.

SALTED CARAMEL
TREATS

No one can resist salted caramel! It's amazing in chocolates, ice cream, pudding, and these fantastic treats. A little salty, perfectly sweet—what's not to love? • **MAKES 16 LARGE OR 24 SMALL BARS**

7 tablespoons unsalted butter

½ cup store-bought caramel sauce

½ teaspoon pure vanilla extract

½ teaspoon fine sea salt

24 Vanilla Marshmallows (page 14) or 1 (16-ounce) bag store-bought marshmallows or 15 ounces marshmallow Fluff

6 cups puffed rice cereal

1 Using 1 tablespoon of the butter, grease the bottom and sides of a 9 x 13-inch glass or nonstick baking dish.

2 In a medium pan set over medium heat, melt the remaining 6 tablespoons butter. Add the caramel sauce, vanilla, and salt, and stir until smooth. Add the marshmallows, reduce the heat to low, and cover the pan. Let stand until the marshmallows begin to soften, 2 minutes. Fold in the cereal and stir gently.

3 Scrape the mixture into the prepared dish and spread evenly with a piece of wax paper. Let stand for 15 minutes before cutting and serving.

DULCE DE LECHE
TREATS

Dulce de leche is a combination of milk and sugar that has been slowly cooked until the sugar caramelizes, producing a thick, creamy, intensely flavored spread that is simply magnificent. While it's good enough eaten by the spoonful, it's truly decadent in a treat.

• MAKES 16 LARGE OR 24 SMALL BARS

7 tablespoons unsalted butter

24 Vanilla Marshmallows (page 14) or 1 (16-ounce) bag store-bought marshmallows or 15 ounces marshmallow Fluff

½ cup dulce de leche

1 teaspoon pure vanilla extract

Pinch of sea salt

6 cups puffed rice cereal

1 Using 1 tablespoon of the butter, grease the bottom and sides of a 9 x 13-inch glass or nonstick baking dish.

2 In a medium pan set over medium heat, melt the remaining 6 tablespoons butter. Add the marshmallows, reduce the heat to low, and cover the pan. Let stand until the marshmallows begin to soften, 2 minutes. Add the dulce de leche, vanilla, and salt, and stir until smooth. Fold in the cereal and stir gently.

3 Scrape the mixture into the prepared dish and spread evenly with a piece of wax paper. Let stand for 15 minutes before cutting and serving.

BROWN BUTTER-VANILLA BEAN
TREATS

Beurre noisette, or brown butter, is a transformative ingredient. With its nutty, caramel flavors that are the result of cooking butter until it turns a fragrant golden brown, it enriches everything it touches. These treats have a touch of sophistication, and all the usual fun.

• **MAKES 16 LARGE OR 24 SMALL BARS**

7 tablespoons unsalted butter

1 vanilla bean, seeds scraped

Pinch of sea salt

24 Vanilla Marshmallows (page 14) or 1 (16-ounce) bag store-bought marshmallows or 15 ounces marshmallow Fluff

6 cups puffed rice cereal

1 Using 1 tablespoon of the butter, grease the bottom and sides of a 9 x 13-inch glass or nonstick baking dish.

2 In a medium pan set over medium heat, melt the remaining 6 tablespoons butter. Cook until the butter turns a deep golden brown, about 4 minutes. Add the vanilla seeds and salt, and stir until smooth. Add the marshmallows, reduce the heat to low, and cover the pan. Let stand until the marshmallows begin to soften, 2 minutes. Fold in the cereal and stir gently.

3 Scrape the mixture into the prepared dish and spread evenly with a piece of wax paper. Let stand for 15 minutes before cutting and serving.

CHOCOLATE-ESPRESSO
TREATS

Coffee and chocolate go together like peanut butter and jelly, or like macaroni and cheese, or like, well, crispy rice cereal and marshmallows! Consider this a decadent, crunchy new pick-me-up dessert. • **MAKES 16 LARGE OR 24 SMALL BARS**

7 tablespoons unsalted butter

1 teaspoon instant espresso powder

½ teaspoon pure vanilla extract

Pinch of sea salt

24 Vanilla Marshmallows (page 14) or 1 (16-ounce) bag store-bought marshmallows or 15 ounces marshmallow Fluff

6 cups chocolate-flavored puffed rice cereal

¾ cup coarsely chopped chocolate-covered espresso beans

1 Using 1 tablespoon of the butter, grease the bottom and sides of a 9 x 13-inch glass or nonstick baking dish.

2 In a medium pan set over medium heat, melt the remaining 6 tablespoons butter. Add the espresso powder, vanilla, and salt, and stir until smooth. Add the marshmallows, reduce the heat to low, and cover the pan. Let stand until the marshmallows begin to soften, 2 minutes. Fold in the cereal and espresso beans, and stir gently.

3 Scrape the mixture into the prepared dish and spread evenly with a piece of wax paper. Let stand for 15 minutes before cutting and serving.

CANDY STORE FAVORITES

CHOCOLATE,
CARAMEL, AND PEANUT TREATS

Is there a better combination than chocolate, peanuts, and caramel? The combination that makes Snickers one of the most popular candy bars also makes a mighty fine marshmallow treat. If you prefer yours less chocolaty, substitute regular rice cereal for the chocolate-flavored variety. • MAKES 16 LARGE OR 24 SMALL BARS

½ cup semisweet or bittersweet chocolate chips

6 tablespoons unsalted butter

24 Vanilla Marshmallows (page 14) or 1 (16-ounce) bag store-bought marshmallow or 15 ounces marshmallow Fluff

¼ cup plus 2 tablespoons store-bought caramel

1 teaspoon pure vanilla extract

Pinch of sea salt

6 cups chocolate-flavored puffed rice cereal

½ cup chopped salted cocktail peanuts

1 Put the chocolate in a microwave-safe bowl and microwave on medium heat in 20-second intervals, stirring after each, until melted and smooth.

2 Using 1 tablespoon of the butter, grease the bottom and sides of a 9 x 13-inch glass or nonstick baking dish.

3 In a medium pan set over medium heat, melt the remaining 5 tablespoons butter. Add the marshmallows, reduce the heat to low, and cover the pan. Let stand until the marshmallows soften, 2 minutes. Add ¼ cup of the caramel, the vanilla, and salt, and stir until smooth. Fold in the cereal and stir gently.

4 Scrape the mixture into the prepared dish and spread evenly with a piece of wax paper. Drizzle with the melted chocolate and the remaining 2 tablespoons caramel, and top with the peanuts. Let stand for 15 minutes before cutting and serving.

CHOCOLATE-COVERED STRAWBERRY

TREATS

Who doesn't love a luscious ripe strawberry dipped in dark chocolate? It is one of my favorite sweets to enjoy, especially with a glass of Champagne when I am feeling decadent. I suggest serving these treats with a big steaming mug of freshly brewed coffee instead.

• MAKES 16 LARGE OR 24 SMALL BARS

7 tablespoons unsalted butter

24 Strawberry Marshmallows (page 17) or 1 (16-ounce) bag store-bought strawberry-flavored marshmallows

Pinch of sea salt

6 cups puffed rice cereal

¾ cup semisweet chocolate chips

¾ cup milk chocolate chips

1 teaspoon canola oil

1 cup finely crushed dehydrated strawberries

1 Using 1 tablespoon of the butter, grease the bottom and sides of a 9 x 13-inch glass or nonstick baking dish.

2 In a medium pan set over medium heat, melt the remaining 6 tablespoons butter. Add the marshmallows, reduce the heat to low, and cover the pan. Let stand until the marshmallows soften, 2 minutes. Fold in the salt and cereal and stir gently.

3 Scrape the mixture into the prepared dish and spread evenly with a piece of wax paper. Let stand for 15 minutes before cutting into 16 large or 24 small bars.

4 Line a baking sheet with parchment paper or wax paper.

5 Combine the chocolate chips in a microwave-safe bowl and melt according to directions on page 11. Whisk in the oil. Let cool for 5 minutes.

6 Drizzle the chocolate over the top of the treats. Dip each bar halfway in the chocolate, let the excess drip off, and put them on the prepared baking sheet. Sprinkle the tops with the crushed strawberries. Refrigerate until the chocolate sets, about 10 minutes, before serving.

CHOCOLATE-CARAMEL
MALTED
TREATS

Chocolate, caramel, and malt powder mix together for a flavor that's reminiscent of the Milky Way candy bar. I love the taste of malt, which is a little toasty and sweet, and it nicely pumps up the flavor of these delicious treats. • **MAKES 16 LARGE OR 24 SMALL BARS**

7 tablespoons unsalted butter

20 fun-size Milky Way candy bars

2 teaspoons malt powder

1 teaspoon pure vanilla extract

Pinch of sea salt

24 Vanilla Marshmallows (page 14) or 1 (16-ounce) bag store-bought marshmallows

6 cups puffed rice cereal

1 Using 1 tablespoon of the butter, grease the bottom and sides of a 9 x 13-inch glass or nonstick baking dish.

2 Finely chop 6 of the candy bars and set aside. Coarsely chop the remaining 14 bars.

3 In a medium pan set over medium heat, melt the remaining 6 tablespoons butter. Add the malt powder, vanilla, and salt, and stir until smooth. Add the marshmallows and the 14 coarsely chopped candy bars, reduce the heat to low, and cover the pan. Let stand until the marshmallows soften, 2 minutes. Fold in the cereal and the 6 finely chopped candy bars, and stir gently.

4 Scrape the mixture into the prepared dish and spread evenly with a piece of wax paper. Let stand for 15 minutes before cutting and serving.

PEANUT BUTTER CUP
TREATS

One of America's favorite candies, now in treat form! Children and adults alike adore peanut butter cups—peanut butter and chocolate is a classic combination that never fails to please.

• MAKES 16 LARGE OR 24 SMALL BARS

7 tablespoons unsalted butter

24 Vanilla Marshmallows (page 14) or 1 (16-ounce) bag store-bought marshmallows or 15 ounces marshmallow Fluff

6 cups puffed rice cereal

1 teaspoon pure vanilla extract

Pinch of sea salt

1½ cups creamy peanut butter (do not use natural peanut butter)

⅓ cup confectioners' sugar

¾ cup semisweet chocolate chips

1 teaspoon vegetable or canola oil

1 Using 1 tablespoon of the butter, grease the bottom and sides of a 9 x 13-inch glass or nonstick baking dish.

2 In a medium pan set over medium heat, melt the remaining 6 tablespoons butter.

Add the marshmallows, reduce the heat to low, and cover the pan. Let stand until the marshmallows soften, 2 minutes. Fold in the cereal, vanilla, and salt, and stir gently.

3 Scrape the mixture into the prepared dish; spread evenly with a piece of wax paper.

4 In a medium bowl, combine the peanut butter and confectioners' sugar. Spread the mixture evenly over the top of the treats and put the dish in the refrigerator to chill for at least 15 minutes and up to 45 minutes.

5 In a microwave-safe bowl, combine the chocolate and oil. Microwave in 20-second intervals, stirring in between, until melted. Pour over the chilled treats. Let stand until the chocolate hardens, 10 minutes, before cutting and serving.

PUPPY CHOW
PRETZEL TREATS

One of my favorite snacks to make and eat is Puppy Chow, which is Rice Chex cereal coated in a melted mixture of chocolate and peanut butter, and then coated in powdered sugar. I thought the concept was perfect for treats, and decided to add some pretzels for an extra crunchy, salty kick. • MAKES 88 PIECES

6 tablespoons unsalted butter

¾ cup semisweet chocolate chips

¾ cup creamy peanut butter (do not use natural peanut butter)

24 Vanilla Marshmallows (page 14) or 1 (16-ounce) bag marshmallows or 15 ounces marshmallow Fluff

1 teaspoon pure vanilla extract

Pinch of sea salt

6 cups puffed rice cereal

1 cup coarsely crushed pretzels

2 cups confectioners' sugar

1 Using 1 tablespoon of the butter, grease the bottom and sides of a 9 x 13-inch glass or nonstick baking dish.

2 In a medium pan set over medium heat, melt the remaining 5 tablespoons butter. Add the chocolate and peanut butter, and stir until smooth. Add the marshmallows, reduce the heat to low, and cover the pan. Let stand until the marshmallows soften, 2 minutes. Fold in the vanilla, salt, cereal, and pretzels, and stir gently.

3 Scrape the mixture into the prepared dish and spread evenly with a piece of wax paper. Refrigerate until chilled, about 15 minutes. Cut the treats into 1-inch bars.

4 Sift the confectioners' sugar into a bowl and toss the treats in the sugar until well coated. Serve.

TREATS BARK
WITH NUTS & DRIED FRUIT

Chocolate bark, with its mix of dried fruits and nuts nestled into rich chocolate, is a yummy treat that's a favorite holiday dessert. Play around with the combination of add-ins. With all that dried fruit and nuts, you can sort of pretend it's a healthy snack. • **MAKES 12 PIECES**

3 tablespoons unsalted butter

15 Vanilla Marshmallows (page 14) or
   8 ounces store-bought marshmallows
   or 8 ounces marshmallow Fluff

1 teaspoon pure vanilla extract

3 cups puffed rice cereal

2½ cups chocolate chips (milk, semisweet,
   or bittersweet)

1 tablespoon canola or vegetable oil

½ cup chopped pistachios or toasted
   almonds

¼ cup chopped dried apricots

¼ cup dried cranberries or cherries

1 Line a sheet pan or small baking sheet with a nonstick baking mat or parchment paper sprayed with nonstick spray.

2 In a medium pan set over low heat, melt the butter. Add the marshmallows and vanilla, cover the pan, and let stand until softened. Fold in the cereal and stir gently.

3 Spread out the mixture on the prepared baking sheet. Use a piece of wax paper and a well-greased spatula to press it into a very thin layer.

4 Melt the chocolate and oil according to the directions on page 11. Stir with a wooden spoon until smooth and let cool, stirring constantly, for about 2 minutes. Pour the chocolate over the top of the treats and spread it into an even layer. Immediately sprinkle the nuts and dried fruit evenly over the top. Refrigerate until the chocolate is set, at least 1 hour, before cutting or breaking the treats into pieces and serving.

ROCKY ROAD
TREATS

Rocky road is a classic ice cream flavor that never goes out of style. The combination of marshmallow, nuts, and chocolate is perfect in treat form. If you can't find chocolate-flavored marshmallows, the regular vanilla flavor will work well, too. • **MAKES 16 LARGE OR 24 SMALL BARS**

7 tablespoons unsalted butter

24 Chocolate Marshmallows (page 20) or 1 (16-ounce) bag store-bought chocolate-flavored marshmallows

1 teaspoon pure vanilla extract

Pinch of sea salt

6 cups chocolate-flavored puffed rice cereal

¾ cup mini marshmallows

½ cup chopped walnuts, almonds, or peanuts

1 Using 1 tablespoon of the butter, grease the bottom and sides of a 9 x 13-inch glass or nonstick baking dish.

2 In a medium pan set over medium heat, melt the remaining 6 tablespoons butter. Add the marshmallows, reduce the heat to low, and cover the pan. Let stand until the marshmallows soften, 2 minutes. Add the vanilla and salt, and stir until smooth. Fold in the cereal, mini marshmallows, and nuts, and stir gently.

3 Scrape the mixture into the prepared dish and spread evenly with a piece of wax paper. Let stand for 15 minutes before cutting and serving.

SALTED CARAMEL & PRETZEL
TREATS

A traditional French confection, salted caramel is now found on every restaurant dessert menu. • **MAKES 16 LARGE OR 24 SMALL BARS**

6 tablespoons unsalted butter

24 Vanilla Marshmallows (page 14) or 1 (16-ounce) bag store-bought marshmallows or 15 ounces marshmallow Fluff

½ cup store-bought caramel

1 teaspoon pure vanilla extract

6 cups puffed rice cereal

1 cup finely crushed pretzels, plus ½ cup coarsely crushed pretzels

1 ounce milk or semisweet chocolate, melted (see page 11)

Flaked sea salt

1 Using 1 tablespoon of the butter, grease the bottom and sides of a 9 x 13-inch glass or nonstick baking dish.

2 In a medium pan set over medium heat, melt the remaining 5 tablespoons butter. Add the marshmallows, reduce the heat to low, and cover the pan. Let stand until the marshmallows soften, 2 minutes. Add ¼ cup of the caramel and the vanilla, and stir until smooth. Fold in the cereal and finely crushed pretzels, and stir gently.

3 Scrape the mixture into the prepared dish and spread evenly with a piece of wax paper. Drizzle with the remaining ¼ cup caramel and the melted chocolate. Sprinkle with the ½ cup coarsely crushed pretzels and a little salt. Let stand for 15 minutes before cutting and serving.

S'MORE
TREATS

Why do I love s'mores so much? There is something about the combination of crispy graham crackers, melted chocolate, and toasted marshmallow that I can't resist. This version is much less messy to eat, and it requires no fire. For extra gooeyness, add some toasted marshmallows on top! · **MAKES 16 LARGE OR 24 SMALL BARS**

24 Vanilla Marshmallows (page 14) or 1 (16-ounce) bag store-bought marshmallows

7 tablespoons unsalted butter

4 cups puffed rice cereal

2 cups Golden Grahams cereal

Pinch of sea salt

1 cup semisweet chocolate chips

1 Put a rack in the upper third of the oven and preheat the broiler. Line a baking sheet with parchment paper. Put half the marshmallows on the baking sheet in an even layer. Broil the marshmallows until golden brown, about 40 seconds. Turn over the marshmallows and brown the other side. Remove from the oven and let cool slightly.

2 Using 1 tablespoon of the butter, grease the bottom and sides of a 9 x 13-inch glass or nonstick baking dish.

3 In a medium pan set over medium heat, melt the remaining 6 tablespoons butter. Add the remaining untoasted marshmallows, reduce the heat to low, and cover the pan. Let stand until the marshmallows soften, 2 minutes. Add the toasted marshmallows, cover the pan, and let stand until halfway melted, 2 minutes. Fold in both cereals, the salt, and ¾ cup of the chocolate chips, and stir gently.

4 Scrape the mixture into the prepared dish and spread evenly with a piece of wax paper. Sprinkle the remaining ¼ cup chocolate chips over the top. Let stand for 15 minutes before cutting and serving.

TURTLE
TREATS

My mother's favorite candy was the turtle. I loved how the round disk of chocolate-covered caramel was supposed to be the body and the four pecans its feet. Making your own caramel is super simple, but feel free to substitute a good-quality prepared brand. • **MAKES 16 LARGE OR 24 SMALL BARS**

CARAMEL

6 tablespoons unsalted butter

1 cup packed light brown sugar

2 tablespoons heavy cream

1 teaspoon pure vanilla extract

TREATS

7 tablespoons unsalted butter

1 teaspoon pure vanilla extract

Pinch of sea salt

24 Vanilla Marshmallows (page 14) or 1 (16-ounce) bag store-bought marshmallows or 15 ounces marshmallow Fluff

6 cups puffed rice cereal

½ cup toasted pecans, coarsely chopped

½ cup milk chocolate chips

1 Make the caramel: In a small saucepan set over medium-high heat, melt the butter. Whisk in the brown sugar and cook, whisking constantly, until the mixture thickens and darkens slightly, about 5 minutes. Add the cream and vanilla, and cook 1 more minute. Remove the pan from the heat and let cool slightly.

2 Make the treats: Using 1 tablespoon of the butter, grease the bottom and sides of a 9 x 13-inch glass or nonstick baking dish.

3 In a medium pan set over medium heat, melt the remaining 6 tablespoons butter. Add the vanilla and salt, and stir until smooth. Add the marshmallows, reduce the heat to low, and cover the pan. Let stand until the marshmallows soften, 2 minutes. Fold in the cereal and stir gently.

4 Scrape the mixture into the prepared dish and spread evenly with a piece of wax paper. Immediately spread the caramel over the top of the treats, and scatter the pecans and the chocolate over the caramel. Refrigerate for 15 minutes to let the caramel set slightly before cutting and serving.

FRUITY SWEETS

BERRY COBBLER
TREATS

Nothing says summer like a berry cobbler! Feel free to substitute any other berry preserves for the strawberry. · **MAKES 16 LARGE OR 24 SMALL BARS**

6 tablespoons unsalted butter

1 vanilla bean, seeds scraped

Pinch of sea salt

24 Strawberry Marshmallows (page 17) or 1 (16-ounce) bag store-bought strawberry-flavored marshmallows

6 cups puffed rice cereal

½ cup strawberry preserves

1 cup plain granola or strawberry granola

1 Using 1 tablespoon of the butter, grease the bottom and sides of a 9 x 13-inch glass or nonstick baking dish.

2 In a medium pan set over medium heat, melt the remaining 5 tablespoons butter. Add the vanilla seeds and salt, and stir until smooth. Add the marshmallows, reduce the heat to low, and cover the pan. Let stand until the marshmallows begin to soften, 2 minutes. Fold in the cereal and stir gently.

3 Scrape the mixture into the prepared dish and spread evenly with a piece of wax paper.

4 Put the preserves and 1 tablespoon of water in a small saucepan and heat over low heat until just warmed through, about 5 minutes. Spread the preserves over the top of the treats and immediately sprinkle the granola over the top. Let stand for 15 minutes before cutting and serving.

ORANGE CREAM
TREATS

Orange sherbet and vanilla ice cream separately are good, but combine the two and suddenly you have a fantastic flavor combination, which has been immortalized in the Creamsicle ice pop. Using fresh orange zest instead of extract makes all the difference, so don't skip it! • **MAKES 16 LARGE OR 24 SMALL BARS**

7 tablespoons unsalted butter

1 teaspoon pure vanilla extract

2 teaspoons finely grated orange zest

24 Vanilla Marshmallows (page 14) or 1 (16-ounce) bag store-bought marshmallows or 15 ounces marshmallow Fluff

6 cups puffed rice cereal

Pinch of salt

1 Using 1 tablespoon of the butter, grease the bottom and sides of a 9 x 13-inch glass or nonstick baking dish.

2 In a medium pan set over medium heat, melt the remaining 6 tablespoons butter. Add the vanilla and orange zest, and stir until smooth. Add the marshmallows, reduce the heat to low, and cover the pan. Let stand until the marshmallows soften, 2 minutes. Fold in the cereal and salt, and stir gently.

3 Scrape the mixture into the prepared dish and spread evenly with a piece of wax paper. Let stand for 15 minutes. Cut and serve.

STRAWBERRY LEMONADE
TREATS

This may be the most girly-girl recipe in the book. I love these pink-tinged treats with lemony drizzle over the top. They're perfect for a ladies-who-lunch get-together or a bake sale at your child's school. • **MAKES 16 LARGE OR 24 SMALL BARS**

6 tablespoons unsalted butter

24 Strawberry Marshmallows (page 17) or 1 (16-ounce) bag store-bought strawberry-flavored marshmallows

Finely grated zest of 1 lemon

Pinch of fine salt

6 cups puffed rice cereal

½ cup dehydrated strawberries, coarsely chopped

¾ cup confectioners' sugar

1 to 2 tablespoons fresh lemon juice

1 Using 1 tablespoon of the butter, grease the bottom and sides of a 9 x 13-inch glass or nonstick baking dish.

2 In a medium pan set over medium heat, melt the remaining 5 tablespoons butter. Add the marshmallows, reduce the heat to low, and cover the pan. Let stand until the marshmallows soften, 2 minutes. Add the lemon zest and salt, and stir until smooth. Fold in the cereal and strawberries, and stir gently.

3 Scrape the mixture into the prepared dish and spread evenly with a piece of wax paper. Let stand for 15 minutes.

4 In a small bowl, whisk together the confectioners' sugar and lemon juice until smooth. Drizzle the glaze over the top. Let stand for 15 more minutes before cutting and serving.

RASPBERRY
CHEESECAKE TREATS

We all know strawberry cheesecake, but other berries pair perfectly with the creamy, lemony tang of a cheesecake filling. My favorite is raspberry, so I made these treats with those. Feel free to substitute the berry you like best. • **MAKES 16 LARGE OR 24 SMALL BARS**

5 tablespoons butter

20 Vanilla Marshmallows (page 14) or
** 12 ounces store-bought marshmallows**
** or 12 ounces marshmallow Fluff**

2 teaspoons pure vanilla extract

3 cups puffed rice cereal

6 graham crackers, finely crushed

1 (8-ounce) package Philadelphia cream
** cheese, room temperature**

1 (14-ounce) can sweetened condensed
** milk**

1 teaspoon finely grated lemon zest

Juice of 1 lemon

3 tablespoons seedless raspberry jam

1 pint fresh ripe raspberries

1 Using 1 tablespoon of the butter, grease the bottom and sides of a 9 x 13-inch glass or nonstick baking dish.

2 In a medium pan set over medium heat, melt the remaining 4 tablespoons butter. Add the marshmallows, reduce the heat to low, and cover the pan. Let stand until the marshmallows soften, 2 minutes. Add 1 teaspoon of vanilla, and stir until smooth. Fold in the cereal and graham crackers, and stir gently.

3 Scrape the mixture into the prepared dish and spread evenly with a piece of wax paper. Let stand for 10 minutes.

4 Meanwhile, whisk together the cream cheese, condensed milk, lemon zest and juice, and the remaining 1 teaspoon vanilla. Spread the mixture over the top of the cooled treats and refrigerate until set, about 4 hours.

5 In a small saucepan set over medium heat, combine the jam and 2 tablespoons of water and cook until heated through. Arrange the raspberries on top of the cheesecake layer, open-side down. Brush the berries and the treats with the melted jam. Cut and serve immediately.

KEY LIME PIE
TREATS

Key lime pie is such a dreamy dessert, and these treats capture the taste surprisingly well. A graham cracker crust and lime filling are topped with lots of creamy marshmallow-like whipped cream. Using fresh limes in this recipe is key to getting the best flavor. • **MAKES 16 LARGE OR 24 SMALL BARS**

7 tablespoons unsalted butter

Finely grated zest of 2 limes

Juice of 1 lime

24 Vanilla Marshmallows (page 14) or 1 (16-ounce) bag store-bought marshmallow or 15 ounces marshmallow Fluff

1 vanilla bean, seeds scraped, or 1 teaspoon pure vanilla extract

Pinch of sea salt

6 cups puffed rice cereal

3 graham crackers, broken into small pieces, or 1 cup Golden Grahams cereal

1 Using 1 tablespoon of the butter, grease the bottom and sides of a 9 x 13-inch glass or nonstick baking dish.

2 In a medium pan set over medium heat, melt the remaining 6 tablespoons butter. Add the lime zest and juice and cook, stirring, for 30 seconds. Add the marshmallows, reduce the heat to low, and cover the pan. Let stand until the marshmallows soften, 2 minutes. Add the vanilla and salt, and stir until smooth. Fold in the cereal and graham crackers, and stir gently.

3 Scrape the mixture into the prepared dish and spread evenly with a piece of wax paper. Let stand for 15 minutes before cutting and serving.

LEMON-POPPY SEED TREATS

I love lemon anything, and lemon–poppy seed muffins are one of my favorites for breakfast. This is my new favorite breakfast treat—it can't be that much worse for you than a muffin! Using fresh lemon zest and juice makes all the difference in the world, so don't substitute extract or the juice in a plastic lemon. • **MAKES 16 LARGE OR 24 SMALL BARS**

7 tablespoons unsalted butter

Finely grated zest of 1 lemon

Juice of 1 lemon

24 Vanilla Marshmallows (page 14) or 1 (16-ounce) bag store-bought marshmallow or 15 ounces marshmallow Fluff

Pinch of sea salt

6 cups puffed rice cereal

2 teaspoons poppy seeds

½ cup confectioners' sugar

1 Using 1 tablespoon of the butter, grease the bottom and sides of a 9 x 13-inch glass or nonstick baking dish.

2 In a medium pan set over medium heat, melt the remaining 6 tablespoons butter. Add the lemon zest and half the juice and cook, stirring, for 30 seconds. Add the marshmallows, reduce the heat to low, and cover the pan. Let stand until the marshmallows soften, 2 minutes. Fold in the salt, cereal, and poppy seeds, and stir gently.

3 Scrape the mixture into the prepared dish and spread evenly with a piece of wax paper. Let stand for 15 minutes.

4 Whisk together the confectioners' sugar and the remaining lemon juice. Drizzle the glaze over the treats. Let stand for another 15 minutes before cutting and serving.

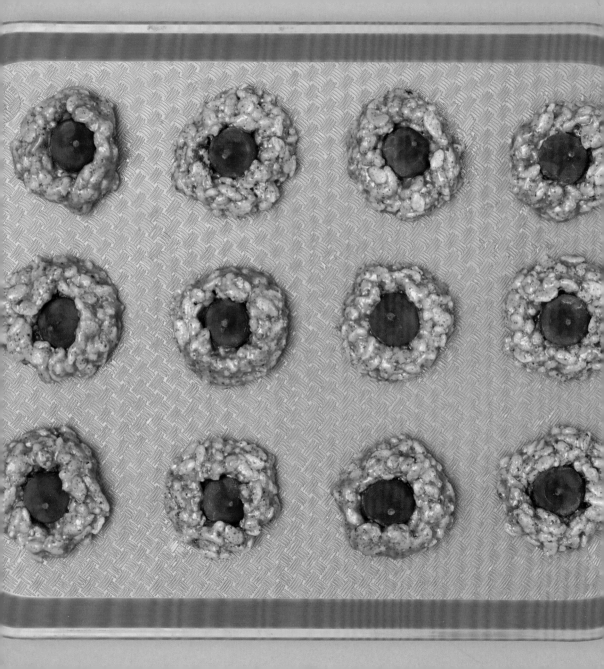

CHOCOLATE DELIGHTS

BLACK & WHITE
TREATS

The black & white is a New York City born-and-raised sponge-like cookie with vanilla and chocolate fondant icing. It is about as iconic as the Empire State Building. These treats don't look much like the cookie, but their taste will remind you of the original. • **MAKES 16 LARGE OR 24 SMALL BARS**

7 tablespoons unsalted butter

24 chocolate wafer cookies (such as Nabisco Famous)

24 Vanilla Marshmallows (page 14) or 1 (16-ounce) bag store-bought marshmallows or 15 ounces marshmallow Fluff

Pinch of sea salt

6 cups chocolate-flavored puffed rice cereal

1 Using 1 tablespoon of the butter, grease the bottom and sides of a 9 x 13-inch glass or nonstick baking dish.

2 Put 15 of the cookies in a food processor and pulse until finely chopped (or put the cookies in a plastic ziptop bag, seal tightly, and crush with a rolling pin). Cut the remaining cookies into quarters. Set aside.

3 In a medium pan set over medium heat, melt the remaining 6 tablespoons butter. Add the marshmallows, reduce the heat to low, and cover the pan. Let stand until the marshmallows soften, 2 minutes. Fold in the salt, cereal, and cookie crumbs, and stir gently.

4 Scrape the mixture into the prepared dish and spread evenly with a piece of wax paper. Immediately press the cookie quarters into the top of the treats. Let stand for 15 minutes before cutting and serving.

MINT CHOCOLATE
TREATS

My favorite Girl Scout cookie is the Thin Mint. My favorite movie theater treat is Junior Mints. My favorite ice cream is Mint–Chocolate Chip. This variety of treat was inevitable.

• MAKES 16 LARGE OR 24 SMALL BARS

7 tablespoons unsalted butter

24 chocolate mint cookies (such as Mint-Chocolate Oreos or Thin Mints)

24 Vanilla Marshmallows (page 14) or 1 (16-ounce) bag store-bought marshmallows or 15 ounces marshmallow Fluff

Pinch of sea salt

6 cups puffed rice cereal

1 Using 1 tablespoon of the butter, grease the bottom and sides of a 9 x 13-inch glass or nonstick baking dish.

2 Put 15 of the cookies in a food processor and pulse until finely chopped (or put the cookies in a plastic ziptop bag, seal tightly, and crush with a rolling pin). Cut the remaining cookies into quarters. Set aside.

3 In a medium pan set over medium heat, melt the remaining 6 tablespoons butter. Add the marshmallows, reduce the heat to low, and cover the pan. Let stand until the marshmallows soften, 2 minutes. Fold in the salt, cereal, and cookie crumbs.

4 Scrape the mixture into the prepared dish and spread evenly with a piece of wax paper. Immediately press the cookie quarters into the top of the treats. Let stand for 15 minutes before cutting and serving.

BLACKOUT
TREATS

You want chocolate? You got it! These bars are ridiculously rich and chocolaty, and perfect with a tall glass of ice-cold milk. I dare you to eat just one! • **MAKES 16 LARGE OR 24 SMALL BARS**

7 tablespoons unsalted butter

½ teaspoon pure vanilla extract

Pinch of sea salt

24 Chocolate Marshmallows (page 20) or 1 (16-ounce) bag store-bought chocolate-flavored marshmallows

6 cups chocolate-flavored puffed rice cereal

15 chocolate wafer cookies (such as Nabisco Famous), coarsely chopped

1 Using 1 tablespoon of the butter, grease the bottom and sides of a 9 x 13-inch glass or nonstick baking dish.

2 In a medium pan set over medium heat, melt the remaining 6 tablespoons butter. Add the vanilla and salt, and stir until smooth. Add the marshmallows, reduce the heat to low, and cover the pan. Let stand until the marshmallows soften, 2 minutes. Fold in the cereal and stir gently.

3 Scrape the mixture into the prepared dish and spread evenly with a piece of wax paper. Immediately sprinkle the cookies evenly over the top, then gently press them into the mixture. Let stand for 15 minutes before cutting and serving.

COOKIES
& CREAM
TREATS

I think the first time I had the combination of cookies and cream was in an ice cream cone— rich vanilla ice cream studded with pieces of chocolate sandwich cookies. It's still one of my favorite flavors. This treat plays on that taste combination, but it will not melt all over your dress on a hot summer day. • **MAKES 16 LARGE OR 24 SMALL BARS**

6 tablespoons unsalted butter

24 chocolate sandwich cookies (such as Oreos or Hydrox)

24 Vanilla Marshmallows (page 14) or 1 (16-ounce) bag store-bought marshmallows or 15 ounces marshmallow Fluff

½ teaspoon pure vanilla extract

Pinch of sea salt

6 cups puffed rice cereal

1 Using 1 tablespoon of the butter, grease the bottom and sides of a 9 x 13-inch glass or nonstick baking dish.

2 Put 15 of the cookies in a food processor and pulse until finely chopped (or put the cookies in a plastic ziptop bag, seal tightly, and crush with a rolling pin). Coarsely chop the remaining 9 cookies. Set aside.

3 In a medium pan set over medium heat, melt the remaining 5 tablespoons butter. Add the marshmallows, reduce the heat to low, and cover the pan. Let stand until the marshmallows soften, 2 minutes. Fold in the vanilla, salt, cereal, and cookie crumbs, and stir gently.

4 Scrape the mixture into the prepared dish and spread evenly with a piece of wax paper. Immediately sprinkle the chopped cookies over the top of the treats. Let stand for 15 minutes before cutting and serving.

ALMOND BLOSSOMS

Another childhood treat turned into a rice cereal variation, but no mixer or oven needed. These are perfect little goodies to serve at a summer party or to make with kids on a rainy afternoon. • **MAKES 26 TO 30 TREATS**

½ **cup corn syrup**

½ **cup sugar**

¾ **cup almond butter**

2 **cups puffed rice cereal**

26 to 30 Hershey's Almond Kisses, **unwrapped**

1 In a heavy large saucepan, bring the corn syrup and sugar to a boil and cook until the sugar has dissolved, 5 minutes. Remove the pan from heat. Add the almond butter and stir quickly until the mixture is smooth and creamy. Fold in the cereal and stir gently.

2 Using a small to medium ice cream scoop, drop small balls of the mixture onto a piece of wax paper. Press down on the middle of each ball with your thumb, and then press a Hershey's Kiss in the indention. Let cool completely before serving.

VARIATION

Peanut Butter Jam Blossoms: Substitute peanut butter for the almond butter and ½ cup strawberry, raspberry, or grape jam for the chocolate Kisses.

CRUNCHY CASHEW
BUCKEYES

I grew up in Pennsylvania, right next to the Buckeye State (also known as Ohio). Peanut butter buckeyes were always a part of our holiday cookie platter. This recipe stays true to my childhood version, but I switched things up and used cashew butter. Pistachio or almond butter would work perfectly, too. • **MAKES 36 BUCKEYES**

2 ounces Philadelphia cream cheese, room temperature

1½ cups crunchy cashew butter

¼ teaspoon pure vanilla extract

1 cup puffed rice cereal, finely crushed

3 cups confectioners' sugar

10 tablespoons unsalted butter, melted and cooled

1 (12-ounce) bag milk, semisweet, or bittersweet chocolate, melted (see page 11)

2 teaspoons canola oil

1 cup finely chopped cashews

1 Line a baking sheet with parchment or wax paper; set aside.

2 In the bowl of a stand mixer fitted with the paddle attachment, beat the cream cheese, cashew butter, and vanilla until smooth. Add the cereal, confectioners' sugar, and butter, and mix until combined. Using a medium ice cream scoop, drop small balls of the mixture on the prepared baking sheet.

3 In a small bowl, combine the melted chocolate and oil. Stick a toothpick into the top of each ball, then dip each ball halfway into the chocolate. Dip the bottoms of the balls in the nuts. Return the balls to the baking sheet. Refrigerate until the chocolate is set, about 15 minutes.

CRUNCHY PEANUT BUTTER
BUCKEYES

Buckeye candy (also referred to simply as buckeyes) is named for its resemblance to the nut of the Ohio buckeye tree. This candy is native to Ohio and can be found in every chocolate store there. I have been making this confection since I was a little girl in my mother's kitchen. I got to roll the balls, which was a big deal. I am all grown up and still love this treat, but I think I love it even more with the crispy addition of rice cereal. • MAKES 32 BUCKEYES

1½ cups peanut butter, crunchy or creamy

4 tablespoons unsalted butter, room temperature

1 cup confectioners' sugar

½ teaspoon pure vanilla extract

2 cups puffed rice cereal

1 (12-ounce) bag semisweet chocolate chips

1 tablespoon vegetable shortening

1 Line a baking sheet with parchment or wax paper; set aside.

2 In the bowl of a stand mixer fitted with the whisk attachment, beat the peanut butter and butter until smooth. Add the confectioners' sugar and vanilla, and beat until fluffy, 2 minutes. Fold in the cereal, and stir gently.

RECIPE CONTINUES

3 Using a small ice cream scoop or tablespoon, scoop out small balls of the mixture. Roll them between your hands until they are round. Put the balls on the prepared baking sheet and refrigerate until chilled, about 30 minutes.

4 Put the chocolate in a microwave-safe bowl and microwave according to the directions on page 11. Once melted, stir in the shortening.

5 Remove the baking sheet from the refrigerator. Stick a toothpick into the top of each ball, then dip each ball halfway into the chocolate. Return the balls to the baking sheet. Refrigerate to set the chocolate, about 15 minutes.

6 The cookies can be stored in an airtight container in the refrigerator for up to two weeks. For best taste and texture, bring them to room temperature before serving.

HOLIDAY & CELEBRATION TREATS

GINGERBREAD
TREATS

I love gingerbread cookies, but truth be told, I can't stand all the work that goes into making those little dolled-up men. Here is my solution, which captures all of that great flavor and crunch in about one-tenth the time. • **MAKES 16 LARGE OR 24 SMALL BARS**

7 tablespoons unsalted butter

16 gingersnap cookies

¼ teaspoon pumpkin pie spice

24 Vanilla Marshmallows (page 14) or 1 (16-ounce) bag store-bought marshmallows or 15 ounces marshmallow Fluff

1 teaspoon pure vanilla extract

Pinch of sea salt

6 cups puffed rice cereal

1 ounce good quality white chocolate, melted (see page 11)

1 Using 1 tablespoon of the butter, grease the bottom and sides of a 9 x 13-inch glass or nonstick baking dish.

2 Put 8 of the cookies in a food processor and pulse until finely chopped (or put the cookies in a plastic ziptop bag, seal tightly, and crush with a rolling pin). Coarsely chop the remaining 8 cookies.

3 In a medium pan set over medium heat, melt the remaining 6 tablespoons butter. Stir in the pumpkin pie spice and cook for a few seconds. Add the crushed cookies and cook for 10 seconds. Add the marshmallows, reduce the heat to low, and cover the pan. Let stand until the marshmallows soften, 2 minutes. Add the vanilla and salt, and stir until smooth. Fold in the cereal and chopped cookies.

4 Scrape the mixture into the prepared dish and spread evenly with a piece of wax paper. Refrigerate for 15 minutes before drizzling with white chocolate. Let stand another 15 minutes before cutting and serving.

SNICKERDOODLE
TREATS

Crispy cinnamony snickerdoodles remind me of the holidays, when we usually baked them. This version captures all the nostalgia. • **MAKES 16 LARGE OR 24 SMALL BARS**

6 tablespoons unsalted butter

½ teaspoon cinnamon

24 Vanilla Marshmallows (page 14) or 1 (16-ounce) bag store-bought marshmallows or 15 ounces marshmallow Fluff

1 teaspoon pure vanilla extract

Pinch of fine salt

6 cups puffed rice cereal

ICING

¾ cup confectioners' sugar

2 tablespoons unsalted butter, melted and cooled

1 tablespoon whole milk

¼ teaspoon ground cinnamon

1 Make the treats: Using 1 tablespoon of the butter, grease the bottom and sides of a 9 x 13-inch glass or nonstick baking dish.

2 In a medium pan set over medium heat, melt the remaining 5 tablespoons butter. Add the cinnamon and cook, stirring, for 10 seconds. Add the marshmallows, reduce the heat to low, and cover the pan. Let stand until the marshmallows soften, 2 minutes. Add the vanilla and salt, and stir until smooth. Fold in the cereal.

3 Scrape the mixture into the prepared dish and spread evenly with a piece of wax paper. Refrigerate for 15 minutes.

4 Make the icing: In a small bowl, whisk together the confectioners' sugar, butter, milk, and cinnamon. Add more milk if needed to reach desired consistency. Drizzle the icing over the top of the treats, and let stand another 15 minutes before cutting and serving.

MAPLE, BROWN SUGAR &
PECAN
TREATS

There is no better flavor, in my opinion, than pure maple syrup. I am one of those people who orders pancakes with my maple syrup, not the other way around. I swear I could drink it by the glassful (and probably have). I recommend using the real stuff for this recipe. Products labeled "pancake syrup" are just artificially flavored corn syrup. These treats are perfect for a Halloween party. • **MAKES 16 LARGE OR 24 SMALL BARS**

7 tablespoons unsalted butter

¼ cup light brown sugar

¼ cup pure Grade B maple syrup

24 Vanilla Marshmallows (page 14) or 1 (16-ounce) bag store-bought marshmallows or 15 ounces marshmallow Fluff

1 teaspoon pure vanilla extract

Pinch of sea salt

6 cups puffed rice cereal

½ cup toasted chopped pecans

1 Using 1 tablespoon of the butter, grease the bottom and sides of a 9 x 13-inch glass or nonstick baking dish.

2 In a medium pan set over medium heat, melt the remaining 6 tablespoons butter. Whisk in the brown sugar and maple syrup. Add the marshmallows, reduce the heat to low, and cover the pan. Let stand until the marshmallows soften, 2 minutes. Add in the vanilla and salt, and stir until smooth. Fold in the cereal and pecans, and stir gently.

3 Scrape the mixture into the prepared dish and spread evenly with a piece of wax paper. Let stand for 15 minutes before cutting and serving.

VANILLA
BIRTHDAY CAKE
TREATS

I believe it all started with ice cream, and then the next thing we knew, there was birthday cake–flavored everything: cupcakes, Oreos, and even M&M's. Now it's time for a treat! The confetti-colored appearance makes these sweets especially celebratory. (See photo, page 84.) • **MAKES 16 LARGE OR 24 SMALL BARS**

7 tablespoons unsalted butter

1 teaspoon pure vanilla extract

Pinch of sea salt

24 Vanilla Marshmallows (page 14) or 1 (16-ounce) bag store-bought marshmallows or 15 ounces marshmallow Fluff

6 cups puffed rice cereal

¼ cup colored candied sprinkles

1 Using 1 tablespoon of the butter, grease the bottom and sides of a 9 x 13-inch glass or nonstick baking dish.

2 In a medium pan set over medium heat, melt the remaining 6 tablespoons butter. Cook until the butter turns a deep golden brown, 2 minutes. Add the vanilla and salt, and stir until smooth. Add the marshmallows, reduce the heat to low, and cover the pan. Let stand until the marshmallows soften, 2 minutes. Fold in the cereal and half of the sprinkles, and stir gently.

3 Scrape the mixture into the prepared dish and spread evenly with a piece of wax paper. Top with the remaining sprinkles. Let stand for 15 minutes before cutting and serving.

WHITE CHOCOLATE-CRANBERRY
TREATS

White chocolate has a natural affinity for cranberry. I think that's because white chocolate is so sweet and cranberries so tart, they balance each other beautifully. While this treat would be great served at any time of year, I always think of cranberries around Thanksgiving and Christmas because their color is so festive. • MAKES 16 LARGE OR 24 SMALL BARS

6 tablespoons unsalted butter

24 Vanilla Marshmallows (page 14) or 1 (16-ounce) bag store-bought marshmallows or 15 ounces marshmallow Fluff

1 teaspoon pure vanilla extract

Pinch of fine salt

6 cups puffed rice cereal

1 cup good-quality white chocolate chips

½ cup dried cranberries or cherries

1 Using 1 tablespoon of the butter, grease the bottom and sides of a 9 x 13-inch glass or nonstick baking dish.

2 In a medium pan set over medium heat, melt the remaining 5 tablespoons butter. Add the marshmallows, reduce the heat to low, and cover the pan. Let stand until the marshmallows soften, 2 minutes. Add the vanilla and salt, and stir until smooth. Fold in the cereal, white chocolate, and dried cranberries, and stir gently.

3 Scrape the mixture into the prepared dish and spread evenly with a piece of wax paper. Let stand for 15 minutes before cutting and serving.

CHOCOLATE-POTATO CHIP
TREATS

Chocolate-covered pretzels have been around forever, or so it seems. A few years ago, I started seeing chocolate-covered potato chips in specialty candy stores, and I immediately fell in love. This recipe is an homage to one of my new favorite salty-chocolate treats.

• **MAKES 16 LARGE OR 24 SMALL BARS**

7 tablespoons unsalted butter

Pinch of sea salt

24 Vanilla Marshmallows (page 14) or 1 (16-ounce) bag store-bought marshmallows or 15 ounces marshmallow Fluff

1 teaspoon pure vanilla extract

4 cups puffed rice cereal

2 cups coarsely crushed ruffled potato chips

1 cup milk or semisweet chocolate chips, melted (see page 11) and slightly cooled

1 Using 1 tablespoon of the butter, grease the bottom and sides of a 9 x 13-inch glass or nonstick baking dish.

2 In a medium pan set over medium heat, melt the remaining 6 tablespoons butter. Add the salt and the marshmallows, reduce the heat to low, and cover the pan. Let stand until the marshmallows soften, 2 minutes. Add the vanilla, and stir until smooth. Fold in the cereal and potato chips, and stir gently.

3 Scrape the mixture into the prepared dish and spread evenly with a piece of wax paper. Let stand for 15 minutes. Drizzle the top with the melted chocolate. Let stand another 15 minutes before cutting and serving.

NEW YORK CHERRY
CHEESECAKE
TREATS

New York City is one of the greatest food meccas in the world, and you can find just about anything you want day or night. One of its most iconic food items is New York–style cheesecake. Its rich and creamy lemon-scented filling is usually topped with cherries or strawberries. For these treats, my Cream Cheese Marshmallows (page 22) lend that tangy kick that all good cheesecakes need. • **MAKES 16 LARGE OR 24 SMALL BARS**

¾ cup dried cherries

6 tablespoons unsalted butter

30 Cream Cheese Marshmallows (page 22)

Finely grated zest of 1 lemon

½ teaspoon pure vanilla extract

Pinch of sea salt

6 cups puffed rice cereal

1 Bring 1 cup of water to a boil. Remove the pan from the heat, add the cherries, and let steep for 30 minutes. Drain the cherries; set aside.

2 Using 1 tablespoon of the butter, grease the bottom and sides of a 9 x 13-inch glass or nonstick baking dish.

3 In a medium pan set over medium heat, melt the remaining 5 tablespoons butter. Add the marshmallows, reduce the heat to low, and cover the pan. Let stand until the marshmallows soften, 2 minutes. Add the lemon zest, vanilla, and salt, and stir until smooth. Fold in the cereal and cherries, and stir gently.

4 Scrape the mixture into the prepared dish and spread evenly with a piece of wax paper. Let stand for 15 minutes before cutting and serving.

INDEX